For all the girls out there. Be bold! Be brave! -H.D.

Text © 2021 Hayley Diep

Illustrations © 2021 Braden Hallett

Printed in the U.S.A. All rights reserved.

ISBN: 978-0-578-75775-9 (hardcover edition)

ISBN: 978-0-578-75744-5 (paperback edition)

Library of Congress Control Number: 2020924544

No part of this publication may be reproduced, stored in a retrieval system, photocopied, recorded or transmitted, in any form or by any means, without the prior written permission of Hayley Diep.

IF YOU GIVE A GIRL A BIKE

By Hayley Diep   Illustrated by Braden Hallett

If you give a girl a bike, and a helmet to go with it, she will ride...

She will climb up hills and shred down mountains.

Occasionally, she will tumble and scrape her knees.

But don't worry! She won't stay down for long.
There are too many places for her to explore.

If you give a girl a skateboard, she will skate...

and skate...

and skate.

But don't worry! She won't stay down for long.
There are too many tricks for her to learn.

She will want to learn how to ollie,

kickflip,

and grind rails.

Sometimes, she will slip and fall onto a mat.

But don't worry! She won't stay down for long. There are too many routes for her to send.

She will carve and ride party waves.

Now and then, she will wipe out.

She will want to barrel ride, nose ride, and practice aerials.

Hayley Diep

Hayley Diep writes and teaches in the Bay Area. When she isn't doing either, you can usually find her reading a book, mountain biking, rock climbing, or riding her longboard with her husband and friends. This book would not have been possible without the support of her husband, family, and friends!
You can follow her at www.hayleydiep.com.

Braden Hallett

Braden loves drawing kids doin' active crazy things and getting into all kinds of trouble. So, really, this book was a dream project. Braden spends his days standing in front of his tablet and doodling.
Find more of Braden's art at www.bradenhallett.com

CPSIA information can be obtained
at www.ICGtesting.com
Printed in the USA
BVHW021508110321
602275BV00006B/49